T
biographies

Malchus, St. Hilarion and Paulus the First Hermit

Saint Jerome

book published by LIMOVIA.NET

**TWITTER:
@EBOOKLIMOVIA**

isbn: 978-1489580153

The LORD said to Moses, "Speak to the entire assembly of Israel and say to them: 'Be holy because I, the LORD your God, am holy. "'Each of you must respect your mother and father, and you must observe my Sabbaths. I am the LORD your God.

Leviticus 19:1,3

Copyright: © 2013 limovia.net - All rights reserved

the author:

Saint Jerome (Latin: Eusebius Sophronius Hieronymus; Greek: Εὐσέβιος Σωφρόνιος Ἱερώνυμος; c. 347 – 30 September 420) is an ancient Latin Christian priest, confessor, theologian and historian, and who became a Doctor of the Church. Though often considered exclusively a saint of the Roman Catholic Church, Jerome was a Latin Christian who predated the East-West Schism which occurred in the 11th century. He was the son of Eusebius, of the city of Stridon, which was on the border of Dalmatia and Pannonia. He is best known for his translation of the Bible into Latin (the Vulgate), and his commentaries on the Gospel of the Hebrews. His list of writings is extensive.

He is recognised by the Catholic Church, the Eastern Orthodox Church, the Lutheran Church, and the Church of England (Anglican

Communion) as a saint. Jerome is commemorated on 30 September with a memorial.

the Vitae Patrum (Vita Pauli primi eremitae), a biography of Saint Paul of Thebes;

the Vita Malchi monachi captivi (ca. 391), probably based on an earlier work, although it purports to be derived from the oral communications of the aged ascetic Malchus originally made to him in the desert of Chalcis;

✓ *the Vita Hilarionis, of the same date, containing more trustworthy historical matter than the other two, and based partly on the biography of Epiphanius and partly on oral tradition.*

Index biogragie

Index

The life of Malchus, the captive Monk......7

The Life of St. Hilarion...........................22

The Life of Paulus the First Hermit........73

Three biographies - Saint Jerome

The life of Malchus, the captive Monk

1. They who have to fight a naval battle prepare for it in harbours and calm waters by adjusting the helm, plying the oars, and making ready the hooks and grappling irons. They draw up the soldiers on the decks and accustom them to stand steady with poised foot and on slippery ground; so that they may not shrink from all this when the real encounter comes, because they have had experience of it in the sham fight. And so it is in my case. I have long held my peace, because silence was imposed on me by one to whom I give pain when I speak of him. But now, in preparing to write history on a wider scale I desire to practise myself by means of this little work and as it were to wipe the rust from my tongue. For I have purposed (if God grant me life, and if my censurers will at length cease to persecute me, now that I am a fugitive and shut up in a monastery) to write a history of the church of Christ from the advent of our Saviour up to our own age, that is from the apostles to the dregs of time in which we live, and to show by

what means and through what agents it received its birth, and how, as it gained strength, it grew by persecution and was crowned with martyrdom; and then, after reaching the Christian Emperors, how it increased in influence and in wealth but decreased in Christian virtues. But of this elsewhere. Now to the matter in hand.

2. Maronia is a little hamlet some thirty miles to the east of Antioch in Syria. After having many owners or landlords, at the time when I was staying as a young man in Syria it came into the possession of my intimate friend, the Bishop Evagrius, whose name I now give in order to show the source of my information. Well, there was at the place at that time an old man by name Malchus, which we might render "king," a Syrian by race and speech, in fact a genuine son of the soil. His companion was an old woman very decrepit who seemed to be at death's door, both of them so zealously pious and such constant frequenters of the Church, they might have been taken for Zacharias and Elizabeth in the Gospel but for the fact that there was no John to be seen. With some curiosity I asked the neighbours what was the link between them; was it marriage, or kindred, or the bond of the Spirit? All with one

accord replied that they were holy people, well pleasing to God, and gave me a strange account of them. Longing to know more I began to question the man with much eagerness about the truth of what I heard, and learned as follows.

3. My son, said he, I used to farm a bit of ground at Nisibis and was an only son. My parents regarding me as the heir and the only survivor of their race, wished to force me into marriage, but I said I would rather be a monk. How my father threatened and my mother coaxed me to betray my chastity requires no other proof than the fact that I fled from home and parents. I could not go to the East because Persia was close by and the frontiers were guarded by the soldiers of Rome; I therefore turned my steps to the West, taking with me some little provision for the journey, but barely sufficient to ward off destitution. To be brief, I came at last to the desert of Chalcis which is situate between Immæ and Beroa farther south. There, finding some monks, I placed myself under their direction, earning my livelihood by the labour of my hands, and curbing the wantonness of the flesh by fasting. After many years the desire came over me to return to my country, and stay with my mother and cheer her

widowhood while she lived (for my father, as I had already heard, was dead), and then to sell the little property and give part to the poor, settle part on the monasteries and (I blush to confess my faithlessness) keep some to spend in comforts for myself. My abbot began to cry out that it was a temptation of the devil, and that under fair pretexts some snare of the old enemy lay hid. It was, he declared, a case of the dog returning to his vomit. Many monks, he said, had been deceived by such suggestions, for the devil never showed himself openly. He set before me many examples from the Scriptures, and told me that even Adam and Eve in the beginning had been overthrown by him through the hope of becoming gods. When he failed to convince me he fell upon his knees and besought me not to forsake him, nor ruin myself by looking back after putting my hand to the plough. Unhappily for myself I had the misfortune to conquer my adviser. I thought he was seeking not my salvation but his own comfort. So he followed me from the monastery as if he had been going to a funeral, and at last bade me farewell, saying, "I see that you bear the brand of a son of Satan. I do not ask your reasons nor take your excuses. The sheep which forsakes its fellows is at once exposed to the jaws of the wolf."

4. On the road from Beroa to Edessa adjoining the high-way is a waste over which the Saracens roam to and fro without having any fixed abode. Through fear of them travellers in those parts assemble in numbers, so that by mutual assistance they may escape impending danger. There were in my company men, women, old men, youths, children, altogether about seventy persons. All of a sudden the Ishmaelites on horses and camels made an assault upon us, with their flowing hair bound with fillets, their bodies half-naked, with their broad military boots, their cloaks streaming behind them, and their quivers slung upon the shoulders. They carried their bows unstrung and brandished their long spears; for they had come not to fight, but to plunder. We were seized, dispersed, and carried in different directions. I, meanwhile, repenting too late of the step I had taken, and far indeed from gaining possession of my inheritance, was assigned, along with another poor sufferer, a woman, to the service of one and the same owner. We were led, or rather carried, high upon the camel's back through a desert waste, every moment expecting destruction, and suspended, I may say, rather than seated. Flesh half raw was our food, camel's milk

our drink.

5. At length, after crossing a great river we came to the interior of the desert, where, being commanded after the custom of the people to pay reverence to the mistress and her children, we bowed our heads. Here, as if I were a prisoner, I changed my dress, that is, learned to go naked, the heat being so excessive as to allow of no clothing beyond a covering for the loins. Some sheep were given to me to tend, and, comparatively speaking, I found this occupation a comfort, for I seldom saw my masters or fellow slaves. My fate seemed to be like that of Jacob in sacred history, and reminded me also of Moses; both of whom were once shepherds in the desert. I fed on fresh cheese and milk, prayed continually, and sang psalms which I had learned in the monastery. I was delighted with my captivity, and thanked God because I had found in the desert the monk's estate which I was on the point of losing in my country.

6. But no condition can ever shut out the Devil. How manifold past expression are his snares! Hid though I was, his malice found me out. My

master seeing his flock increasing and finding no dishonesty in me (I knew that the Apostle has given command that masters should be as faithfully served as God Himself), and wishing to reward me in order to secure my greater fidelity, gave me the woman who was once my fellow servant in captivity. On my refusing and saying I was a Christian, and that it was not lawful for me to take a woman to wife so long as her husband was alive (her husband had been captured with us, but carried off by another master), my owner was relentless in his rage, drew his sword and began to make at me. If I had not without delay stretched out my hand and taken possession of the woman, he would have slain me on the spot. Well; by this time a darker night than usual had set in and, for me, all too soon. I led my bride into an old cave; sorrow was bride's-maid; we shrank from each other but did not confess it. Then I really felt my captivity; I threw myself down on the ground, and began to lament the monastic state which I had lost, and said: "Wretched man that I am! have I been preserved for this? has my wickedness brought me to this, that in my gray hairs I must lose my virgin state and become a married man? What is the good of having despised parents, country, property, for the Lord's sake, if I do the thing I wished to avoid doing when I despised them? And yet it may be perhaps the case that I am in this condition because I longed for home. What are we to do, my soul? are we to perish, or conquer? Are we to wait for the hand of the Lord, or pierce ourselves with our own sword? Turn your weapon against yourself; I must fear your death, my soul, more than the death of the body. Chastity preserved has its own martyrdom. Let the witness for Christ lie unburied in the desert; I will be at once the persecutor and the martyr." Thus speaking I drew my sword which glittered even in the dark, and turning its point towards me said: "Farewell, unhappy woman: receive me as a martyr not as a husband." She threw herself at my feet and exclaimed: "I pray you by Jesus Christ, and adjure you by this hour of trial, do not shed your blood and bring its guilt upon me. If you choose to die, first turn your sword against me. Let us rather be united upon these terms. Supposing my husband should return to me, I would preserve the chastity which I have learned in captivity; I would even die rather than lose it. Why should you die to prevent a union with me? I would die if you desired it. Take me then as the partner of your chastity; and love me more in this union of the spirit than you could in that of the body only. Let our master believe that you are my husband.

Three biographies - Saint Jerome

Christ knows you are my brother. We shall easily convince them we are married when they see us so loving." I confess, I was astonished and, much as I had before admired the virtue of the woman, I now loved her as a wife still more. Yet I never gazed upon her naked person; I never touched her flesh, for I was afraid of losing in peace what I had preserved in the conflict. In this strange wedlock many days passed away. Marriage had made us more pleasing to our masters, and there was no suspicion of our flight; sometimes I was absent for even a whole month like a trusty shepherd traversing the wilderness.

7. After a long time as I sat one day by myself in the desert with nothing in sight save earth and sky, I began quickly to turn things over in my thoughts, and among others called to mind my friends the monks, and specially the look of the father who had instructed me, kept me, and lost me. While I was thus musing I saw a crowd of ants swarming over a narrow path. The loads they carried were clearly larger than their own bodies. Some with their forceps were dragging along the seeds of herbs: others were excavating the earth from pits and banking it up to keep out the water. One party, in view of approaching winter, and

wishing to prevent their store from being converted into grass through the dampness of the ground, were cutting off the tips of the grains they had carried in; another with solemn lamentation were removing the dead. And, what is stranger still in such a host, those coming out did not hinder those going in; nay rather, if they saw one fall beneath his burden they would put their shoulders to the load and give him assistance. In short that day afforded me a delightful entertainment. So, remembering how Solomon sends us to the shrewdness of the ant and quickens our sluggish faculties by setting before us such an example, I began to tire of captivity, and to regret the monk's cell, and long to imitate those ants and their doings, where toil is for the community, and, since nothing belongs to any one, all things belong to all.

8. When I returned to my chamber, my wife met me. My looks betrayed the sadness of my heart. She asked why I was so dispirited. I told her the reasons, and exhorted her to escape. She did not reject the idea. I begged her to be silent on the matter. She pledged her word. We constantly spoke to one another in whispers; and we floated in suspense between hope and fear. I had in the

flock two very fine he-goats: these I killed, made their skins into bottles, and from their flesh prepared food for the way. Then in the early evening when our masters thought we had retired to rest we began our journey, taking with us the bottles and part of the flesh. When we reached the river which was about ten miles off, having inflated the skins and got astride upon them, we entrusted ourselves to the water, slowly propelling ourselves with our feet, that we might be carried down by the stream to a point on the opposite bank much below that at which we embarked, and that thus the pursuers might lose the track. But meanwhile the flesh became sodden and partly lost, and we could not depend on it for more than three days' sustenance. We drank till we could drink no more by way of preparing for the thirst we expected to endure, then hastened away, constantly looking behind us, and advanced more by night than day, on account both of the ambushes of the roaming Saracens, and of the excessive heat of the sun. I grow terrified even as I relate what happened; and, although my mind is perfectly at rest, yet my frame shudders from head to foot.

9. Three days after we saw in the dim distance

two men riding on camels approaching with all speed. At once foreboding ill I began to think my master purposed putting us to death, and our sun seemed to grow dark again. In the midst of our fear, and just as we realized that our footsteps on the sand had betrayed us, we found on our right hand a cave which extended far underground. Well, we entered the cave: but we were afraid of venomous beasts such as vipers, basilisks, scorpions, and other creatures of the kind, which often resort to such shady places so as to avoid the heat of the sun. We therefore barely went inside, and took shelter in a pit on the left, not venturing a step farther, lest in fleeing from death we should run into death. We thought thus within ourselves: If the Lord helps us in our misery we have found safety: if He rejects us for our sins, we have found our grave. What do you suppose were our feelings? What was our terror, when in front of the cave, close by, there stood our master and fellow-servant, brought by the evidence of our footsteps to our hiding place? How much worse is death expected than death inflicted! Again my tongue stammers with distress and fear; it seems as if I heard my master's voice, and I hardly dare mutter a word. He sent his servant to drag us from the cavern while he himself held the camels and, sword in hand, waited for us to

Three biographies - Saint Jerome

come. Meanwhile the servant entered about three or four cubits, and we in our hiding place saw his back though he could not see us, for the nature of the eye is such that those who go into the shade out of the sunshine can see nothing. His voice echoed through the cave: "Come out, you felons; come out and die; why do you stay? Why do you delay? Come out, your master is calling and patiently waiting for you." He was still speaking when lo! through the gloom we saw a lioness seize the man, strangle him, and drag him, covered with blood, farther in. Good Jesus! how great was our terror now, how intense our joy! We beheld, though our master knew not of it, our enemy perish. He, when he saw that he was long in returning, supposed that the fugitives being two to one were offering resistance. Impatient in his rage, and sword still in hand, he came to the cavern, and shouted like a madman as he chided the slowness of his slave, but was seized upon by the wild beast before he reached our hiding place. Who ever would believe that before our eyes a brute would fight for us?

One cause of fear was removed, but there was the prospect of a similar death for ourselves, though the rage of the lion was not so bad to bear as the anger of the man. Our hearts failed for fear:

without venturing to stir a step we awaited the issue, having no wall of defence in the midst of so great dangers save the consciousness of our chastity; when, early in the morning, the lioness, afraid of some snare and aware that she had been seen took up her cub in her teeth and carried it away, leaving us in possession of our retreat. Our confidence was not restored all at once. We did not rush out, but waited for a long time; for as often as we thought of coming out we pictured to ourselves the horror of falling in with her.

10. At last we got rid of our fright; and when that day was spent, we sallied forth towards evening, and saw the camels, on account of their great speed called dromedaries, quietly chewing the cud. We mounted, and with the strength gained from the new supply of grain, after ten days travelling through the desert arrived at the Roman camp. After being presented to the tribune we told all, and from thence were sent to Sabianus, who commanded in Mesopotamia, where we sold our camels. My dear old abbot was now sleeping in the Lord; I betook myself therefore to this place, and returned to the monastic life, while I entrusted my companion here to the care of the virgins; for though I loved her as a sister, I did

not commit myself to her as if she were my sister.

Malchus was an old man, I a youth, when he told me these things. I who have related them to you am now old, and I have set them forth as a history of chastity for the chaste. Virgins, I exhort you, guard your chastity. Tell the story to them that come after, that they may realize that in the midst of swords, and wild beasts of the desert, virtue is never a captive, and that he who is devoted to the service of Christ may die, but cannot be conquered.

The Life of St. Hilarion

1. Before I begin to write the life of the blessed Hilarion I invoke the aid of the Holy Spirit who dwelt in him, that He who bestowed upon the saint his virtues may grant me such power of speech to relate them that my words may be adequate to his deeds. For the virtue of those who have done great deeds is esteemed in proportion to the ability with which it has been praised by men of genius. Alexander the Great of Macedon who is spoken of by Daniel as the ram, or the panther, or the he-goat, on reaching the grave of Achilles exclaimed "Happy Youth! to have the privilege of a great herald of your worth," meaning, of course, Homer. I, however, have to tell the story of the life and conversation of a man so renowned that even Homer were he here would either envy me the theme or prove unequal to it. It is true that that holy man Epiphanius, bishop of Salamis in Cyprus, who had much intercourse with Hilarion, set forth his praises in a short but widely circulated letter. Yet it is one thing to praise the dead in general terms, another to relate their characteristic virtues. And so we in taking up the work begun by him do him service

rather than wrong: we despise the abuse of some who as they once disparaged my hero Paulus, will now perhaps disparage Hilarion; the former they censured for his solitary life; they may find fault with the latter for his intercourse with the world; the one was always out of sight, therefore they think he had no existence; the other was seen by many, therefore he is deemed of no account. It is just what their ancestors the Pharisees did of old! they were not pleased with Matthew 11:18 John fasting in the desert, nor with our Lord and Saviour in the busy throng, eating and drinking. But I will put my hand to the work on which I have resolved, and go on my way closing my ears to the barking of Scylla's hounds.

2. The birth place of Hilarion was the village Thabatha, situate about five miles to the south of Gaza, a city of Palestine. His parents were idolaters, and therefore, as the saying is, the rose blossomed on the thorn. By them he was committed to the charge of a Grammarian at Alexandria, where, so far as his age allowed, he gave proofs of remarkable ability and character: and in a short time endeared himself to all and became an accomplished speaker. More important than all this, he was a believer in the

Lord Jesus, and took no delight in the madness of the circus, the blood of the arena, the excesses of the theatre: his whole pleasure was in the assemblies of the Church.

3. At that time he heard of the famous name of Antony, which was in the mouth of all the races of Egypt. He was fired with a desire to see him, and set out for the desert. He no sooner saw him than he changed his former mode of life and abode with him about two months, studying the method of his life and the gravity of his conduct: his assiduity in prayer, his humility in his dealings with the brethren, his severity in rebuke, his eagerness in exhortation. He noted too that the saint would never on account of bodily weakness break his rule of abstinence or deviate from the plainness of his food. At last, unable to endure any longer the crowds of those who visited the saint because of various afflictions or the assaults of demons, and deeming it a strange anomaly that he should have to bear in the desert the crowds of the cities, he thought it was better for him to begin as Antony had begun. Said he: "Antony is reaping the reward of victory like a hero who has proved his bravery. I have not entered on the soldier's career." He therefore returned with

Three biographies - Saint Jerome

certain monks to his country, and, his parents being now dead, gave part of his property to his brothers, part to the poor, keeping nothing at all for himself, for he remembered with awe the passage in the Acts of the Apostles and dreaded the example and the punishment of Ananias and Sapphira; above all he was mindful of the Lord's words, Luke 14:33 "whosoever he be of you that renounces not all that he has, he cannot be my disciple." At this time he was about fifteen years old. Accordingly, stripped bare and armed with the weapons of Christ, he entered the wilderness which stretches to the left seven miles from Majoma, the port of Gaza, as you go along the coast to Egypt. And although the locality had a record of robbery and of blood, and his relatives and friends warned him of the danger he was incurring, he despised death that he might escape death.

4. His courage and tender years would have been a marvel to all, were it not that his heart was on fire and his eyes bright with the gleams and sparks of faith. His cheeks were smooth, his body thin and delicate, unfit to bear the slightest injury which cold or heat could inflict. What then? With no other covering for his limbs but a shirt of

sackcloth, and a cloak of skins which the blessed Antony had given him when he set out, and a blanket of the coarsest sort, he found pleasure in the vast and terrible wilderness with the sea on one side and the marshland on the other. His food was only fifteen dried figs after sunset. And because the district was notorious for brigandage, it was his practice never to abide long in the same place. What was the devil to do? Whither could he turn? He who once boasted and said, Isaiah 14:14 "I will ascend into heaven, I will set my throne above the stars of the sky, I will be like the most High," saw himself conquered and trodden under foot by a boy whose years did not allow of sin.

5. Satan therefore tickled his senses and, as is his wont, lighted in his maturing body the fires of lust. This mere beginner in Christ's school was forced to think of what he knew not, and to revolve whole trains of thought concerning that of which he had no experience. Angry with himself and beating his bosom (as if with the blow of his hand he could shut out his thoughts) "Ass!" he exclaimed, "I'll stop your kicking, I will not feed you with barley, but with chaff. I will weaken you with hunger and thirst, I will

lade you with heavy burdens, I will drive you through heat and cold, that you may think more of food than wantonness." So for three or four days afterwards he sustained his sinking spirit with the juice of herbs and a few dried figs, praying frequently and singing, and hoeing the ground that the suffering of fasting might be doubled by the pain of toil. At the same time he wove baskets of rushes and emulated the discipline of the Egyptian monks, and put into practice the Apostle's precept, 2 Thessalonians 3:10 "If any will not work, neither let him eat." By these practices he became so enfeebled and his frame so wasted, that his bones scarcely held together.

6. One night he began to hear the wailing of infants, the bleating of flocks, the lowing of oxen, the lament of what seemed to be women, the roaring of lions, the noise of an army, and moreover various portentous cries which made him in alarm shrink from the sound ere he had the sight. He understood that the demons were disporting themselves, and falling on his knees he made the sign of the cross on his forehead. Thus armed as he lay he fought the more bravely, half longing to see those whom he shuddered to hear,

and anxiously looking in every direction. Meanwhile all at once in the bright moonlight he saw a chariot with dashing steeds rushing upon him. He called upon Jesus, and suddenly before his eyes, the earth was opened and the whole array was swallowed up. Then he said, Exodus 15:1 "The horse and his rider has He thrown into the sea." And, "Some trust in chariots, and some in horses; but we will triumph in the name of the Lord our God."

7. So many were his temptations and so various the snares of demons night and day, that if I wished to relate them, a volume would not suffice. How often when he lay down did naked women appear to him, how often sumptuous feasts when he was hungry! Sometimes as he prayed a howling wolf sprang past or a snarling fox, and when he sang a gladiatorial show was before him, and a man newly slain would seem to fall at his feet and ask him for burial.

8. Once upon a time he was praying with his head upon the ground. As is the way with men, his attention was withdrawn from his devotions, and he was thinking of something else, when a

Three biographies - Saint Jerome

tormentor sprang upon his back and driving his heels into his sides and beating him across the neck with a horse-whip cried out "Come! why are you asleep?" Then with a loud laugh asked if he was tired and would like to have some barley.

9. From his sixteenth to his twentieth year he shielded himself from heat and rain in a little hut which he had constructed of reeds and sedge. Afterwards he built himself a small cell which remains to the present day, five feet in height, that is less than his own height, and only a little more in length. One might suppose it a tomb rather than a house.

10. He shaved his hair once a year on Easter Day, and until his death was accustomed to lie on the bare ground or on a bed of rushes. The sackcloth which he had once put on he never washed, and he used to say that it was going too far to look for cleanliness in goats' hair-cloth. Nor did he change his shirt unless the one he wore was almost in rags. He had committed the Sacred Writings to memory, and after prayer and singing was wont to recite them as if in the presence of God. It would be tedious to narrate singly the successive

steps of his spiritual ascent; I will therefore set them in a summary way before my reader, and describe his mode of life at each stage, and will afterwards return to proper historical sequence.

11. From his twentieth to his twenty-seventh year, for three years his food was half a pint of lentils moistened with cold water, and for the next three dry bread with salt and water. From his twenty-seventh year onward to the thirtieth, he supported himself on wild herbs and the raw roots of certain shrubs. From his thirty-first to his thirty-fifth year, he had for food six ounces of barley bread, and vegetables slightly cooked without oil. But finding his eyes growing dim and his whole body shrivelled with a scabby eruption and dry mange, he added oil to his former food and up to the sixty-third year of his life followed this temperate course, tasting neither fruit nor pulse, nor anything whatsoever besides. Then when he saw that his bodily health was broken down, and thought death was near, from his sixty-fourth year to his eightieth he abstained from bread. The fervour of his spirit was so wonderful, that at times when others are wont to allow themselves some laxity of living he appeared to be entering like a novice on the service of the Lord. He made

a sort of broth from meal and bruised herbs, food and drink together scarcely weighing six ounces, and, while obeying this rule of diet, he never broke his fast before sunset, not even on festivals nor in severe sickness. But it is now time to return to the course of event.

12. While still living in the hut, at the age of eighteen, robbers came to him by night, either supposing that he had something which they might carry off, or considering that they would be brought into contempt if a solitary boy felt no dread of their attacks. They searched up and down between the sea and the marsh from evening until daybreak without being able to find his resting place. Then, having discovered the boy by the light of day they asked him, half in jest, "What would you do if robbers came to you?" He replied, "He that has nothing does not fear robbers." Said they, "At all events, you might be killed." "I might," said he, "I might; and therefore I do not fear robbers because I am prepared to die." Then they marvelled at his firmness and faith, confessed how they had wandered about in the night, and how their eyes had been blinded, and promised to lead a stricter life in the future.

13. He had now spent twenty-two years in the wilderness and was the common theme in all the cities of Palestine, though everywhere known by repute only. The first person bold enough to break into the presence of the blessed Hilarion was a certain woman of Eleutheropolis who found that she was despised by her husband on account of her sterility (for in fifteen years she had borne no fruit of wedlock). He had no expectation of her coming when she suddenly threw herself at his feet. "Forgive my boldness," she said: "take pity on my necessity. Why do you turn away your eyes? Why shun my entreaties? Do not think of me as a woman, but as an object of compassion. It was my sex that bore the Saviour. Luke 5:31 They that are whole have no need of a physician, but they that are sick." At length, after a long time he no longer turned away, but looked at the woman and asked the cause of her coming and of her tears. On learning this he raised his eyes to heaven and bade her have faith, then wept over her as she departed. Within a year he saw her with a son.

14. This his first miracle was succeeded by another still greater and more notable. Aristæneté

the wife of Elpidius who was afterwards pretorian prefect, a woman well known among her own people, still better known among Christians, on her return with her husband, from visiting the blessed Antony, was delayed at Gaza by the sickness of her three children; for there, whether it was owing to the vitiated atmosphere, or whether it was, as afterwards became clear, for the glory of God's servant Hilarion, they were all alike seized by a semi-tertian ague and despaired of by the physicians. The mother lay wailing, or as one might say walked up and down between the corpses of her three sons not knowing which she should first have to mourn for. When, however, she knew that there was a certain monk in the neighbouring wilderness, forgetting her matronly state (she only remembered she was a mother) she set out accompanied by her handmaids and eunuchs, and was hardly persuaded by her husband to take an ass to ride upon. On reaching the saint she said, "I pray you by Jesus our most merciful God, I beseech you by His cross and blood, to restore to me my three sons, so that the name of our Lord and Saviour may be glorified in the city of the Gentiles. Then shall his servants enter Gaza and the idol Marnas shall fall to the ground." At first he refused and said that he never left his cell and was not accustomed to enter a house, much less the city; but she threw herself upon the ground and cried repeatedly, "Hilarion, servant of Christ, give me back my children: Antony kept them safe in Egypt, do you save them in Syria." All present were weeping, and the saint himself wept as he denied her. What need to say more? the woman did not leave him till he promised that he would enter Gaza after sunset. On coming thither he made the sign of the cross over the bed and fevered limbs of each, and called upon the name of Jesus. Marvellous efficacy of the Name! As if from three fountains the sweat burst forth at the same time: in that very hour they took food, recognized their mourning mother, and, with thanks to God, warmly kissed the saint's hands. When the matter was noised abroad, and the fame of it spread far and wide, the people flocked to him from Syria and Egypt, so that many believed in Christ and professed themselves monks. For as yet there were no monasteries in Palestine, nor had anyone known a monk in Syria before the saintly Hilarion. It was he who originated this mode of life and devotion, and who first trained men to it in that province. The Lord Jesus had in Egypt the aged Antony: in Palestine He had the youthful Hilarion.

15. Facidia is a hamlet belonging to Rhino-Corura, a city of Egypt. From this village a woman who had been blind for ten years was brought to the blessed Hilarion, and on being presented to him by the brethren (for there were now many monks with him) affirmed that she had spent all her substance on physicians. The saint replied: "If you had given to the poor what you have wasted on physicians, the true physician Jesus would have cured you." But when she cried aloud and entreated pity, he spat into her eyes, in imitation of the Saviour, and with similar instant effect.

16. A charioteer, also of Gaza, stricken by a demon in his chariot became perfectly stiff, so that he could neither move his hand nor bend his neck. He was brought on a litter, but could only signify his petition by moving his tongue; and was told that he could not be healed unless he first believed in Christ and promised to forsake his former occupation. He believed, he promised, and he was healed: and rejoiced more in the saving of the soul than in that of the body.

17. Again, a very powerful youth called Marsitas from the neighbourhood of Jerusalem plumed himself so highly on his strength that he carried fifteen bushels of grain for a long time and over a considerable distance, and considered it as his highest glory that he could beat the asses in endurance. This man was afflicted with a grievous demon and could not endure chains, or fetters, but broke even the bolts and bars of the doors. He had bitten off the noses and ears of many: had broken the feet of some, the legs of others. He had struck such terror of himself into everybody, that he was laden with chains and dragged by ropes on all sides like a wild bull to the monastery. As soon as the brethren saw him they were greatly alarmed (for the man was of gigantic size) and told the Father. He, seated as he was, commanded him to be brought to him and released. When he was free, "Bow your head," said he, "and come." The man began to tremble; he twisted his neck round and did not dare to look him in the face, but laid aside all his fierceness and began to lick his feet as he sat. At last the demon which had possessed the young man being tortured by the saint's adjurations came forth on the seventh day.

18. Nor must we omit to tell that Orion, a leading man and wealthy citizen of Aira, on the coast of the Red Sea, being possessed by a legion of demons was brought to him. Hands, neck, sides, feet were laden with iron, and his glaring eyes portended an access of raging madness. As the saint was walking with the brethren and expounding some passage of Scripture the man broke from the hands of his keepers, clasped him from behind and raised him aloft. There was a shout from all, for they feared lest he might crush his limbs wasted as they were with fasting. The saint smiled and said, "Be quiet, and let me have my rival in the wrestling match to myself." Then he bent back his hand over his shoulder till he touched the man's head, seized his hair and drew him round so as to be foot to foot with him; he then stretched both his hands in a straight line, and trod on his two feet with both his own, while he cried out again and again, "To torment with you! ye crowd of demons, to torment!" The sufferer shouted aloud and bent back his neck till his head touched the ground, while the saint said, "Lord Jesus, release this wretched man, release this captive. Yours it is to conquer many, no less than one." What I now relate is unparalleled: from one man's lips were heard different voices and as it were the confused shouts of a multitude.

Well, he too was cured, and not long after came with his wife and children to the monastery bringing many gifts expressive of his gratitude. The saint thus addressed him— "Have you not read what befell Gehazi and Simon, one of whom took a reward, the other offered it, the former in order to sell grace, the latter to buy it?" And when Orion said with tears, "Take it and give it to the poor," he replied, "You can best distribute your own gifts, for you tread the streets of the cities and know the poor. Why should I who have forsaken my own seek another man's? To many the name of the poor is a pretext for their avarice; but compassion knows no artifices. No one better spends than he who keeps nothing for himself." The man was sad and lay upon the ground. "Be not sad, my son," he said; "what I do for my own good I do also for yours. If I were to take these gifts I should myself offend God, and, moreover, the legion would return to you."

19. There is a story relating to Majomites of Gaza which it is impossible to pass over in silence. While quarrying building stones on the shore not far from the monastery he was helplessly paralysed, and after being carried to the saint by his fellow-workman immediately returned to his

work in perfect health. I ought to explain that the shore of Palestine and Egypt naturally consists of soft sand and gravel which gradually becomes consolidated and hardens into rock; and thus though to the eye it remains the same it is no longer the same to the touch.

20. Another story relates to Italicus, a citizen of the same town. He was a Christian and kept horses for the circus to contend against those of the Duumvir of Gaza who was a votary of the idol god Marnas. This custom at least in Roman cities was as old as the days of Romulus, and was instituted in commemoration of the successful seizure of the Sabine women. The chariots raced seven times round the circus in honour of Consus in his character of the God of Counsel. Victory lay with the team which tired out the horses opposed to them. Now the rival of Italicus had in his pay a magician to incite his horses by certain demoniacal incantations, and keep back those of his opponent. Italicus therefore came to the blessed Hilarion and besought his aid not so much for the injury of his adversary as for protection for himself. It seemed absurd for the venerable old man to waste prayers on trifles of this sort. He therefore smiled and said, "Why do

you not rather give the price of the horses to the poor for the salvation of your soul?" His visitor replied that his office was a public duty, and that he acted not so much from choice as from compulsion, that no Christian man could employ magic, but would rather seek aid from a servant of Christ, especially against the people of Gaza who were enemies of God, and who would exult over the Church of Christ more than over him. At the request therefore of the brethren who were present he ordered an earthenware cup out of which he was wont to drink to be filled with water and given to Italicus. The latter took it and sprinkled it over his stable and horses, his charioteers and his chariot, and the barriers of the course. The crowd was in a marvellous state of excitement, for the enemy in derision had published the news of what was going to be done, and the backers of Italicus were in high spirits at the victory which they promised themselves. The signal is given; the one team flies towards the goal, the other sticks fast: the wheels are glowing hot beneath the chariot of the one, while the other scarce catches a glimpse of their opponents' backs as they flit past. The shouts of the crowd swell to a roar, and the heathens themselves with one voice declare Marnas is conquered by Christ. After this the opponents in their rage demanded that Hilarion as a Christian magician should be dragged to execution. This decisive victory and several others which followed in successive games of the circus caused many to turn to the faith.

21. There was a youth in the neighbourhood of the same market-town of Gaza who was desperately in love with one of God's virgins. After he had tried again and again those touches, jests, nods, and whispers which so commonly lead to the destruction of virginity, but had made no progress by these means, he went to a magician at Memphis to whom he proposed to make known his wretched state, and then, fortified with his arts, to return to his assault upon the virgin. Accordingly after a year's instruction by the priest of Æsculapius, who does not heal souls but destroys them, he came full of the lust which he had previously allowed his mind to entertain, and buried beneath the threshold of the girl's house certain magical formulæ and revolting figures engraven on a plate of Cyprian brass. Thereupon the maid began to show signs of insanity, to throw away the covering of her head, tear her hair, gnash her teeth, and loudly call the youth by name. Her intense affection had become

a frenzy. Her parents therefore brought her to the monastery and delivered her to the aged saint. No sooner was this done than the devil began to howl and confess. "I was compelled, I was carried off against my will. How happy I was when I used to beguile the men of Memphis in their dreams! What crosses, what torture I suffer! You force me to go out, and I am kept bound under the threshold. I cannot go out unless the young man who keeps me there lets me go." The old man answered, "Your strength must be great indeed, if a bit of thread and a plate can keep you bound. Tell me, how is it that you dared to enter into this maid who belongs to God?" "That I might preserve her as a virgin," said he. "You preserve her, betrayer of chastity! Why did you not rather enter into him who sent you?" "For what purpose," he answers, "should I enter into one who was in alliance with a comrade of my own, the demon of love?" But the saint would not command search to be made for either the young man or the charms till the maiden had undergone a process of purgation, for fear that it might be thought that the demon had been released by means of incantations, or that he himself had attached credit to what he said. He declared that demons are deceitful and well versed in dissimulation, and sharply rebuked the virgin when she had recovered her health for having by her conduct given an opportunity for the demon to enter.

22. It was not only in Palestine and the neighbouring cities of Egypt or Syria that he was in high repute, but his fame had reached distant provinces. An officer of the Emperor Constantius whose golden hair and personal beauty revealed his country (it lay between the Saxons and the Alemanni, was of no great extent but powerful, and is known to historians as Germany, but is now called France), had long, that is to say from infancy, been pursued by a devil, who forced him in the night to howl, groan, and gnash his teeth. He therefore secretly asked the Emperor for a post-warrant, plainly telling him why he wanted it, and having also obtained letters to the legate at Palestine came with great pomp and a large retinue to Gaza. On his inquiring of the local senators where Hilarion the monk dwelt, the people of Gaza were much alarmed, and supposing that he had been sent by the Emperor, brought him to the monastery, that they might show respect to one so highly accredited, and that, if any guilt had been incurred by them by injuries previously done by them to Hilarion it

might be obliterated by their present dutifulness. The old man at the time was taking a walk on the soft sands and was humming some passage or other from the psalms. Seeing so great a company approaching he stopped, and having returned the salutes of all while he raised his hand and gave them his blessing, after an hour's interval he bade the rest withdraw, but would have his visitor together with servants and officers remain: for by the man's eyes and countenance he knew the cause of his coming. Immediately on being questioned by the servant of God the man sprang up on tiptoe, so as scarcely to touch the ground with his feet, and with a wild roar replied in Syriac in which language he had been interrogated. Pure Syriac was heard flowing from the lips of a barbarian who knew only French and Latin, and that without the absence of a sibilant, or an aspirate, or an idiom of the speech of Palestine. The demon then confessed by what means he had entered into him. Further, that his interpreters who knew only Greek and Latin might understand, Hilarion questioned him also in Greek, and when he gave the same answer in the same words and alleged in excuse many occasions on which spells had been laid upon him, and how he was bound to yield to magic arts, "I care not," said the saint, "how you came

Three biographies - Saint Jerome

to enter, but I command you in the name of our Lord Jesus Christ to come out." The man, as soon as he was healed, with a rough simplicity offered him ten pounds of gold. But the saint took from him only bread, and told him that they who were nourished on such food regarded gold as mire.

23. It is not enough to speak of men; brute animals were also daily brought to him in a state of madness, and among them a Bactrian camel of enormous size amid the shouts of thirty men or more who held him tight with stout ropes. He had already injured many. His eyes were bloodshot, his mouth filled with foam, his rolling tongue swollen, and above every other source of terror was his loud and hideous roar. Well, the old man ordered him to be let go. At once those who brought him as well as the attendants of the saint fled away without exception. The saint went by himself to meet him, and addressing him in Syriac said, "You do not alarm me, devil, huge though your present body is. Whether in a fox or a camel you are just the same." Meanwhile he stood with outstretched hand. The brute raging and looking as if he would devour Hilarion came up to him, but immediately fell down, laid its head on the ground, and to the amazement of all

present showed suddenly no less tameness than it had exhibited ferocity before. But the old man declared to them how the devil, for men's sake, seizes even beasts of burden; that he is inflamed by such intense hatred for men that he desires to destroy not only them but what belongs to them. As an illustration of this he added the fact that before he was permitted to try the saintly Job, he made an end of all his substance. Nor ought it to disturb anyone that by the Lord's command two thousand swine were slain by the agency of demons, since those who witnessed the miracle could not have believed that so great a multitude of demons had gone out of the man unless an equally vast number of swine had rushed to ruin, showing that it was a legion that impelled them.

24. Time would fail me if I wished to relate all the miracles which were wrought by him. For to such a pitch of glory was he raised by the Lord that the blessed Antony among the rest hearing of his life wrote to him and gladly received his letters. And if ever the sick from Syria came to him he would say to them, "Why have you taken the trouble to come so far, when you have there my son Hilarion?" Following his example, however, innumerable monasteries sprang up

throughout the whole of Palestine, and all the monks flocked to him. When he saw this he praised the Lord for His grace, and exhorted them individually to the profit of their souls, telling them that the fashion of this world passes away, and that the true life is that which is purchased by suffering in the present.

25. Wishing to set the monks an example of humility and of zeal he was accustomed on fixed days before the vintage to visit their cells. When the brethren knew this they would all come together to meet him, and in company with their distinguished leader go the round of the monasteries, taking with them provisions, because sometimes as many as two thousand men were assembled. But, as time went on, all the settlements round gladly gave food to the neighbouring monks for the entertainment of the saints. Moreover, the care he took to prevent any brother however humble or poor being passed over is evidenced by the journey which he once took into the desert of Cades to visit one of his disciples. With a great company of monks he reached Elusa, as it happened on the day when the annual festival had brought all the people together to the temple of Venus. This, goddess is

worshipped on account of Lucifer to whom the Saracen nation is devoted. The very town too is to a great extent semi-barbarous, owing to its situation. When therefore it was heard that Saint Hilarion was passing through (he had frequently healed many Saracens possessed by demons), they went to meet him in crowds with their wives and children, bending their heads and crying in the Syriac tongue Barech, that is, Bless. He received them with courtesy and humility, and prayed that they might worship God rather than stones; at the same time, weeping copiously, he looked up to heaven and promised that if they would believe in Christ he would visit them often. By the marvellous grace of God they did not suffer him to depart before he had drawn the outline of a church, and their priest with his garland upon his head had been signed with the sign of Christ.

26. Another year, again, when he was setting out to visit the monasteries and was drawing up a list of those with whom he must stay and whom he must see in passing, the monks knowing that one of their number was a niggard, and being at the same time desirous to cure his complaint, asked the saint to stay with him. He replied, "Do you

wish me to inflict injury on you and annoyance on the brother?" The niggardly brother on hearing of this was ashamed, and with the strenuous support of all his brethren, at length obtained from the saint a reluctant promise to put his monastery on the roll of his resting places. Ten days after they came to him and found the keepers already on guard in the vineyard through which their course lay, to keep off all comers with stones and clods and slings. In the morning they all departed without having eaten a grape, while the old man smiled and pretended not to know what had happened.

27. Once when they were being entertained by another monk whose name was Sabus (we must not of course give the name of the niggard, we may tell that of this generous man), because it was the Lord's day, they were all invited by him into the vineyard so that before the hour for food came they might relieve the toil of the journey by a repast of grapes. Said the saint, "Cursed be he who looks for the refreshment of the body before that of the soul. Let us pray, let us sing, let us do our duty to God, and then we will hasten to the vineyard." When the service was over, he stood on an eminence and blessed the vineyard and let

his own sheep go to their pasture. Now those who partook were not less than three thousand. And whereas the whole vineyard had been estimated at a hundred flagons, within thirty days he made it worth three hundred. The niggardly brother gathered much less than usual, and he was grieved to find that even what he had turned to vinegar. The old man had predicted this to many brethren before it happened. He particularly abhorred such monks as were led by their lack of faith to hoard for the future, and were careful about expense, or raiment, or some other of those things which pass away with the world.

28. Lastly he would not even look at one of the brethren who lived about five miles off because he ascertained that he very jealously guarded his bit of ground, and had a little money. The offender wishing to be reconciled to the old man often came to the brethren, and in particular to Hesychius who was specially dear to Hilarion. One day accordingly he brought a bundle of green chick-pea just as it had been gathered. Hesychius placed it on the table against the evening, whereupon the old man cried out that he could not bear the stench, and asked where it came from. Hesychius replied that a certain

brother had sent the brethren the first fruits of his ground. "Don't you notice," said he, "the horrid stench, and detect the foul odour of avarice in the peas? Send it to the cattle, send to the brute-beasts and see whether they can eat it." No sooner was it in obedience to his command laid in the manger than the cattle in the wildest alarm and bellowing loudly broke their fastenings and fled in different directions. For the old man was enabled by grace to tell from the odour of bodies and garments, and the things which any one had touched, by what demon or with what vice the individual was distressed.

29. His sixty-third year found the old man at the head of a grand monastery and a multitude of resident brethren. There were such crowds of persons constantly bringing those who suffered from various kinds of sickness or were possessed of unclean spirits, that the whole circuit of the wilderness was full of all sorts of people. And as the saint saw all this he wept daily and called to mind with incredible regret his former mode of life. When one of the brethren asked him why he was so dejected he replied, "I have returned again to the world and have received my reward in my lifetime. The people of Palestine and the

adjoining province think me of some importance, and under pretence of a monastery for the well-ordering of the brethren I have all the apparatus of a paltry life about me." The brethren, however, kept watch over him and in particular Hesychius, who had a marvellously devoted affection and veneration for the old man. After he had spent two years in these lamentations Aristæneté the lady of whom we made mention before, as being then the wife of a prefect though without any of a prefect's ostentation, came to him intending to pay a visit to Antony also. He said to her, "I should like to go myself too if I were not kept a prisoner in this monastery, and if my going could be fruitful. For it is now two days since mankind was bereaved of him who was so truly a father to them all." She believed his word and stayed where she was: and after a few days the news came that Antony had fallen asleep.

30. Some may wonder at the miracles he worked, or his incredible fasting, knowledge, and humility. Nothing so astonishes me as his power to tread under foot honour and glory. Bishops, presbyters, crowds of clergymen and monks, of Christian matrons even (a great temptation), and a rabble from all quarters in town and country

were congregating about him, and even judges and others holding high positions, that they might receive at his hands the bread or oil which he had blessed. But he thought of nothing but solitude, so much so that one day he determined to be gone, and having procured an ass (he was almost exhausted with fasting and could scarcely walk) endeavoured to steal away. The news spread far and wide, and, just as if a public mourning for the desolation of Palestine were decreed, ten thousand people of various ages and both sexes came together to prevent his departure. He was unmoved by entreaties, and striking the sand with his stick kept saying: "I will not make my Lord a deceiver; I cannot look upon churches overthrown, Christ's altars trodden down, the blood of my sons poured out." All who were present began to understand that some secret had been revealed to him which he was unwilling to confess, but they none the less kept guard over him that he might not go. He therefore determined, and publicly called all to witness, that he would take neither food nor drink unless he were released. Only after seven days was he relieved from his fasting; when having bidden farewell to numerous friends, he came to Betilium attended by a countless multitude. There he prevailed upon the crowd to return and chose as his companions forty monks who had resources for the journey and were capable of travelling during fasting-time, that is, after sunset. He then visited the brethren who were in the neighbouring desert and sojourning at a place called Lychnos, and after three days came to the castle of Theubatus to see Dracontius, bishop and confessor, who was in exile there. The bishop was beyond measure cheered by the presence of so distinguished a man. At the end of another three days he set out for Babylon and arrived there after a hard journey. Then he visited Philo the bishop, who was also a confessor; for the Emperor Constantius who favoured the Arian heresy had transported both of them to those parts. Departing thence he came in three days to the town Aphroditon. There he met with a deacon Baisanes who kept dromedaries which were hired, on account of the scarcity of water in the desert, to carry travellers who wished to visit Antony. He then made known to the brethren that the anniversary of the blessed Antony's decease was at hand, and that he must spend a whole night in vigil in the very place where the saint had died. So then after three days journey through the waste and terrible desert they at length came to a very high mountain, and there found two monks, Isaac and Pelusianus, the former of whom had been one of Antony's attendants.

31. The occasion seems a fitting one, since we are on the spot itself, to describe the abode of this great man. There is a high and rocky mountain extending for about a mile, with gushing springs among its spurs, the waters of which are partly absorbed by the sand, partly flow towards the plain and gradually form a stream shaded on either side by countless palms which lend much pleasantness and charm to the place. Here the old man might be seen pacing to and fro with the disciples of blessed Antony. Here, so they said, Antony himself used to sing, pray, work, and rest when weary. Those vines and shrubs were planted by his own hand: that garden bed was his own design. This pool for watering the garden was made by him after much toil. That hoe was handled by him for many years. Hilarion would lie upon the saint's bed and as though it were still warm would affectionately kiss it. The cell was square, its sides measuring no more than the length of a sleeping man. Moreover on the lofty mountaintop, the ascent of which was by a zig-zag path very difficult, were to be seen two cells of the same dimensions, in which he stayed when he escaped from the crowds of visitors or the

company of his disciples. These were cut out of the live rock and were only furnished with doors. When they came to the garden, "You see," said Isaac, "this garden with its shrubs and green vegetables; about three years ago it was ravaged by a troop of wild asses. One of their leaders was hidden by Antony to stand still while he thrashed the animal's sides with a stick and wanted to know why they devoured what they had not sown. And ever afterwards, excepting the water which they were accustomed to come and drink, they never touched anything, not a bush or a vegetable." The old man further asked to be shown his burial place, and they thereupon took him aside; but whether they showed him the tomb or not is unknown. It is related that the motive for secrecy was compliance with Antony's orders and to prevent Pergamius, a very wealthy man of the district, from removing the saint's body to his house and erecting a shrine to his memory.

32. Having returned to Aphroditon and keeping with him only two of the brethren, he stayed in the neighbouring desert, and practised such rigid abstinence and silence that he felt that then for the first time he had begun to serve Christ. Three years had now elapsed since the heavens had

Three biographies - Saint Jerome

been closed and the land had suffered from drought, and it was commonly said that even the elements were lamenting the death of Antony. Hilarion did not remain unknown to the inhabitants of that place any more than to others, but men and women with ghastly faces and wasted by hunger earnestly entreated the servant of Christ, as being the blessed Antony's successor, to give them rain. Hilarion when he saw them was strangely affected with compassion and, raising his eyes to heaven and lifting up both his hands, he at once obtained their petition. But, strange to say, that parched and sandy district, after the rain had fallen, unexpectedly produced such vast numbers of serpents and poisonous animals that many who were bitten would have died at once if they had not run to Hilarion. He therefore blessed some oil with which all the husbandmen and shepherds touched their wounds, and found an infallible cure.

33. Seeing that even there surprising respect was paid to him, he went to Alexandria, intending to cross from thence to the farther oasis of the desert. And because he had never stayed in cities since he entered on the monk's life, he turned aside to some brethren at Bruchium, not far from

Alexandria, whom he knew, and who welcomed the old man with the greatest pleasure. It was now night when all at once they heard his disciples saddling the ass and making ready for the journey. They therefore threw themselves at his feet and besought him not to leave them; they fell prostrate before the door, and declared they would rather die than lose such a guest. He answered: "My reason for hastening away is that I may not give you trouble. You will no doubt afterwards discover that I have not suddenly left without good cause." Next day the authorities of Gaza with the lictors of the prefect having heard of his arrival on the previous day, entered the monastery, and when they failed to find him anywhere they began to say to one another: "What we heard is true. He is a magician and knows the future." The fact was that the city of Gaza on Julian's accession to the throne, after the departure of Hilarion from Palestine and the destruction of his monastery, had presented a petition to the Emperor requesting that both Hilarion and Hesychius might be put to death, and a proclamation had been published everywhere that search should be made for them.

34. Having then left Bruchium, he entered the

oasis through the trackless desert, and there abode for a year, more or less. But, inasmuch as his fame had travelled thither also, he felt that he could not be hidden in the East, where he was known to many by report and by sight, and began to think of taking ship for some solitary island, so that having been exposed to public view by the land, he might at least find concealment in the sea. Just about that time Hadrian, his disciple, arrived from Palestine with information that Julian was slain and that a Christian emperor had commenced his reign; he ought therefore, it was said, to return to the relics of his monastery. But he, when he heard this, solemnly refused to return; and hiring a camel crossed the desert waste and reached Paretonium, a city on the coast of Libya. There the ill-starred Hadrian wishing to return to Palestine and unwilling to part with the renown so long attaching to his master's name, heaped reproaches upon him, and at last having packed up the presents which he had brought him from the brethren, set out without the knowledge of Hilarion. As I shall have no further opportunity of referring to this man, I would only record, for the terror of those who despise their masters, that after a little while he was attacked by the king's-evil and turned to a mass of corruption.

35. The old man accompanied by Gazanus went on board a ship which was sailing to Sicily. Half way across the Adriatic he was preparing to pay his fare by selling a copy of the Gospels which he had written with his own hand in his youth, when the son of the master of the ship seized by a demon began to cry out and say: "Hilarion, servant of God, why is it that through you we cannot be safe even on the sea? Spare me a little until I reach land. Let me not be cast out here and thrown into the deep." The saint replied: "If my God permit you to remain, remain; but if He casts you out, why bring odium upon me a sinner and a beggar?" This he said that the sailors and merchants on board might not betray him on reaching shore. Not long after, the boy was cleansed, his father and the rest who were present having given their word that they would not reveal the name of the saint to any one.

36. On approaching Pachynus, a promontory of Sicily, he offered the master the Gospel for the passage of himself and Gazanus. The man was unwilling to take it, all the more because he saw that excepting that volume and the clothes they wore they had nothing, and at last he swore he

would not take it. But the aged saint, ardent and confident in the consciousness of his poverty, rejoiced exceedingly that he had no worldly possessions and was accounted a beggar by the people of the place.

37. Once more, on thinking the matter over and fearing that merchants coming from the East might make him known, he fled to the interior, some twenty miles from the sea, and there on an abandoned piece of ground, every day tied up a bundle of firewood which he laid upon the back of his disciple, and sold at some neighbouring mansion. They thus supported themselves and were able to purchase a morsel of bread for any chance visitors. But that came exactly to pass which is written: Matthew 5:14 "a city set on a hill cannot be hid." It happened that one of the shields-men who was vexed by a demon was in the basilica of the blessed Peter at Rome, when the unclean spirit within him cried out, "A few days ago Christ's servant Hilarion entered Sicily and no one knew him, and he thinks he is hidden. I will go and betray him." Immediately he embarked with his attendants in a ship lying in harbour, sailed to Pachynus and, led by the demon to the old man's hut, there prostrated

himself and was cured on the spot. This, his first miracle in Sicily, brought the sick to him in countless numbers (but it brought also a multitude of religious persons); insomuch that one of the leading men who was swollen with the dropsy was cured the same day that he came. He afterwards offered the saint gifts without end, but the saint replied to him in the words of the Saviour to his disciples: Matthew 10:8 "Freely ye received, freely give."

38. While this was going on in Sicily Hesychius his disciple was searching the world over for the old man, traversing the coast, penetrating deserts, clinging all the while to the belief that wherever he was he could not long be hidden. At the end of three years he heard at Methona from a certain Jew, who dealt in old-clothes, that a Christian prophet had appeared in Sicily, and was working such miracles and signs, one might think him one of the ancient saints. So he asked about his dress, gait, and speech, and in particular his age, but could learn nothing. His informant merely declared that he had heard of the man by report. He therefore crossed the Adriatic and after a prosperous voyage came to Pachynus, where he took up his abode in a cottage on the shore of the

Three biographies - Saint Jerome

bay, and, on inquiring for tidings of the old man, discovered by the tale which every one told him where he was, and what he was doing. Nothing about him surprised them all so much as the fact that after such great signs and wonders he had not accepted even a crust of bread from any one in the district. And, to cut my story short, the holy man Hesychius fell down at his master's knees and bedewed his feet with tears; at length he was gently raised by him, and when two or three days had been spent in talking over matters, he learned from Gazanus that Hilarion no longer felt himself able to live in those parts, but wanted to go to certain barbarous races where his name and fame were unknown.

39. He therefore brought him to Epidaurus, a town in Dalmatia, where he stayed for a few days in the country near, but could not be hid. An enormous serpent, of the sort which the people of those parts call boas because they are so large that they often swallow oxen, was ravaging the whole province far and wide, and was devouring not only flocks and herds, but husbandmen and shepherds who were drawn in by the force of its breathing. He ordered a pyre to be prepared for it, then sent up a prayer to Christ, called forth the

reptile, bade it climb the pile of wood, and then applied the fire. And so before all the people he burnt the savage beast to ashes. But now he began anxiously to ask what he was to do, whither to betake himself. Once more he prepared for flight, and in thought ranged through solitary lands, grieving that his miracles could speak of him though his tongue was silent.

40. At that time there was an earthquake over the whole world, following on the death of Julian, which caused the sea to burst its bounds, and left ships hanging on the edge of mountain steeps. It seemed as though God were threatening a second deluge, or all things were returning to original chaos. When the people of Epidaurus saw this, I mean the roaring waves and heaving waters and the swirling billows mountain-high dashing on the shore, fearing that what they saw had happened elsewhere might befall them and their town be utterly destroyed, they made their way to the old man, and as if preparing for a battle placed him on the shore. After making the sign of the cross three times on the sand, he faced the sea, stretched out his hands, and no one would believe to what a height the swelling sea stood like a wall before him. It roared for a long time as

Three biographies - Saint Jerome

if indignant at the barrier, then little by little sank to its level. Epidaurus and all the region roundabout tell the story to this day, and mothers teach their children to hand down the remembrance of it to posterity. Verily, what was said to the Apostles, "If you have faith, you shall say to this mountain, Remove into the sea, and it shall be done," may be even literally fulfilled, provided one has such faith as the Lord commanded the Apostles to have. For what difference does it make whether a mountain descends into the sea, or huge mountains of waters everywhere else fluid suddenly become hard as rock at the old man's feet?

41. The whole country marvelled and the fame of the great miracle was in everyone's mouth, even at Salonæ. When the old man knew this was the case he escaped secretly by night in a small cutter, and finding a merchant ship after two days came to Cyprus. Between Malea and Cythera, the pirates, who had left on the shore that part of their fleet which is worked by poles instead of sails, bore down on them with two light vessels of considerable size; and besides this they were buffeted by the waves on every side. All the rowers began to be alarmed, to weep, to leave

their places, to get out their poles, and, as though one message was not enough, again and again told the old man that pirates were at hand. Looking at them in the distance he gently smiled, then turned to his disciples and said, Matthew 14:32 "O you of little faith, wherefore do ye doubt? Are these more than the army of Pharaoh? Yet they were all drowned by the will of God." Thus he spoke, but none the less the enemy with foaming prows kept drawing nearer and were now only a stone's throw distant. He stood upon the prow of the vessel facing them with outstretched hand, and said, "Thus far and no farther." Marvellous to relate, the boats at once bounded back, and though urged forward by the oars fell farther and farther astern. The pirates were astonished to find themselves going back, and laboured with all their strength to reach the vessel, but were carried to the shore faster by far than they came.

42. I pass by the rest for fear I should seem in my history to be publishing a volume of miracles. I will only say this, that when sailing with a fair wind among the Cyclades he heard the voices of unclean spirits shouting in all directions from towns and villages, and running in crowds to the

shore. Having then entered Paphos, the city of Cyprus renowned in the songs of the poets, the ruins of whose temples after frequent earthquakes are the only evidences at the present day of its former grandeur, he began to live in obscurity about two miles from the city, and rejoiced in having a few days rest. But not quite twenty days passed before throughout the whole island whoever had unclean spirits began to cry out that Hilarion Christ's servant had come, and that they must go to him with all speed. Salamis, Curium, Lapetha, and the other cities joined in the cry, while many declared that they knew Hilarion and that he was indeed the servant of Christ, but where he was they could not tell. So within a trifle more than thirty days, about two hundred people, both men and women, came together to him. When he saw them he lamented that they would not suffer him to be quiet, and thirsting in a kind of manner to avenge himself, he lashed them with such urgency of prayer that some immediately, others after two or three days, all within a week, were cured.

43. Here he stayed two years, always thinking of flight, and in the meantime sent Hesychius, who was to return in the spring, to Palestine to salute

the brethren and visit the ashes of his monastery. When the latter returned he found Hilarion longing to sail again to Egypt, that is to the locality called Bucolia; but he persuaded him that, since there were no Christians there, but only a fierce and barbarous people, he should rather go to a spot in Cyprus itself which was higher up and more retired. After long and diligent search he found such a place twelve miles from the sea far off among the recesses of rugged mountains, the ascent to which could hardly be accomplished by creeping on hands and knees. Thither he conducted him. The old man entered and gazed around. It was indeed a lonely and terrible place; for though surrounded by trees on every side, with water streaming from the brow of the hill, a delightful bit of garden, and fruit-trees in abundance (of which, however, he never ate), yet it had close by the ruins of an ancient temple from which, as he himself was wont to relate and his disciples testify, the voices of such countless demons re-echoed night and day, that you might have thought there was an army of them. He was highly pleased at the idea of having his opponents in the neighbourhood, and abode there five years, cheered in these his last days by the frequent visits of Hesychius, for owing to the steep and rugged ascent, and the

Three biographies - Saint Jerome

numerous ghosts (so the story ran), nobody or scarcely anybody either could or dared to go up to him. One day, however, as he was leaving his garden, he saw a man completely paralysed lying in front of the gates. He asked Hesychius who he was, or how he had been brought. Hesychius replied that he was the agent at the country-house to which the garden belonged in which they were located. Weeping much and stretching out his hand to the prostrate man he said, "I bid you in the name of our Lord Jesus Christ arise and walk." The words were still on the lips of the speaker, when, with miraculous speed, the limbs were strengthened and the man arose and stood firm. Once this was noised abroad the need of many overcame even the pathless journey and the dangers of the place. The occupants of all the houses round about had nothing so much in their thoughts as to prevent the possibility of his escape, a rumour having spread concerning him to the effect that he could not stay long in the same place. This habit of his was not due to levity or childishness, but to the fact that he shunned the worry of publicity and praise, and always longed for silence and a life of obscurity.

44. In his eightieth year, during the absence of

Hesychius, he wrote by way of a will a short letter with his own hand, and left him all his riches (that is to say, a copy of the gospels, and his sack-cloth tunic, cowl and cloak), for his servant had died a few days before. Many devout men therefore came to the invalid from Paphos, and specially because they had heard of his saying that he must soon migrate to the Lord and must be liberated from the bonds of the body. There came also Constantia a holy woman whose son-in-law and daughter he had anointed with oil and saved from death. He earnestly entreated them all not to let him be kept even a moment of time after death, but to bury him immediately in the same garden, just as he was, clad in his goat-hair tunic, cowl, and his peasant's cloak.

45. His body was now all but cold, and nought was left of life but reason. Yet with eyes wide open he kept repeating, "Go forth, what do you fear? Go forth, my soul, why do you hesitate? You have served Christ nearly seventy years, and do you fear death?" Thus saying he breathed his last. He was immediately buried before the city heard of his death.

46. When the holy man Hesychius heard of his decease, he went to Cyprus and, to lull the suspicions of the natives who were keeping strict guard, pretended that he wished to live in the same garden, and then in the course of about ten months, though at great peril to his life, stole the saint's body. He carried it to Majuma; and there all the monks and crowds of towns-folk going in procession laid it to rest in the ancient monastery. His tunic, cowl and cloak, were uninjured; the whole body as perfect as if alive, and so fragrant with sweet odours that one might suppose it to have been embalmed.

47. In bringing my book to an end I think I ought not to omit to mention the devotion of the holy woman Constantia who, when a message was brought her that Hilarion's body was in Palestine, immediately died, proving even by death the sincerity of her love for the servant of God. For she was accustomed to spend whole nights in vigil at his tomb, and to converse with him as if he were present in order to stimulate her prayers. Even at the present day one may see a strange dispute between the people of Palestine and the Cypriotes, the one contending that they have the body, the other the spirit of Hilarion. And yet in

both places great miracles are wrought daily, but to a greater extent in the garden of Cyprus, perhaps because that spot was dearest to him.

Three biographies - Saint Jerome

The Life of Paulus the First Hermit

1. It has been a subject of wide-spread and frequent discussion what monk was the first to give a signal example of the hermit life. For some going back too far have found a beginning in those holy men Elias and John, of whom the former seems to have been more than a monk and the latter to have begun to prophesy before his birth. Others, and their opinion is that commonly received, maintain that Antony was the originator of this mode of life, which view is partly true. Partly I say, for the fact is not so much that he preceded the rest as that they all derived from him the necessary stimulus. But it is asserted even at the present day by Amathas and Macarius, two of Antony's disciples, the former of whom laid his master in the grave, that a certain Paul of Thebes was the leader in the movement, though not the first to bear the name, and this opinion has my approval also. Some as they think fit circulate stories such as this— that he was a man living in an underground cave with flowing hair down to his feet, and invent many incredible tales which it would be useless to

detail. Nor does the opinion of men who lie without any sense of shame seem worthy of refutation. So then inasmuch as both Greek and Roman writers have handed down careful accounts of Antony, I have determined to write a short history of Paul's early and latter days, more because the thing has been passed over than from confidence in my own ability. What his middle life was like, and what snares of Satan he experienced, no man, it is thought, has yet discovered.

2. During the persecutions of Decius and Valerian, when Cornelius at Rome and Cyprian at Carthage shed their blood in blessed martyrdom, many churches in Egypt and the Thebaid were laid waste by the fury of the storm. At that time the Christians would often pray that they might be smitten with the sword for the name of Christ. But the desire of the crafty foe was to slay the soul, not the body; and this he did by searching diligently for slow but deadly tortures. In the words of Cyprian himself who suffered at his hands: they who wished to die were not suffered to be slain. We give two illustrations, both as specially noteworthy and to make the cruelty of the enemy better known.

Three biographies - Saint Jerome

3. A martyr, steadfast in faith, who stood fast as a conqueror amidst the racks and burning plates, was ordered by him to be smeared with honey and to be made to lie under a blazing sun with his hands tied behind his back, so that he who had already surmounted the heat of the frying-pan might be vanquished by the stings of flies. Another who was in the bloom of youth was taken by his command to some delightful pleasure gardens, and there amid white lilies and blushing roses, close by a gently murmuring stream, while overhead the soft whisper of the wind played among the leaves of the trees, was laid upon a deep luxurious feather-bed, bound with fetters of sweet garlands to prevent his escape. When all had withdrawn from him a harlot of great beauty drew near and began with voluptuous embrace to throw her arms around his neck, and, wicked even to relate! to handle his person, so that when once the lusts of the flesh were roused, she might accomplish her licentious purpose. What to do, and whither to turn, the soldier of Christ knew not. Unconquered by tortures he was being overcome by pleasure. At last with an inspiration from heaven he bit off the end of his tongue and spat it in her face as she

kissed him. Thus the sensations of lust were subdued by the intense pain which followed.

4. While such enormities were being perpetrated in the lower part of the Thebaid, Paul and his newly married sister were bereaved of both their parents, he being about sixteen years of age. He was heir to a rich inheritance, highly skilled in both Greek and Egyptian learning, gifted with a gentle disposition and a deep love for God. Amid the thunders of persecution he retired to a house at a considerable distance and in a more secluded spot. But to what crimes does not the "accursed thirst for gold" impel the human heart? His brother-in-law conceived the thought of betraying the youth whom he was bound to conceal. Neither a wife's tears which so often prevail, nor the ties of blood, nor the all-seeing eye of God above him could turn the traitor from his wickedness. "He came, he was urgent, he acted with cruelty while seeming only to press the claims of affection."

5. The young man had the tact to understand this, and, conforming his will to the necessity, fled to the mountain wilds to wait for the end of the

persecution. He began with easy stages, and repeated halts, to advance into the desert. At length he found a rocky mountain, at the foot of which, closed by a stone, was a cave of no great size. He removed the stone (so eager are men to learn what is hidden), made eager search, and saw within a large hall, open to the sky, but shaded by the wide-spread branches of an ancient palm. The tree, however, did not conceal a fountain of transparent clearness, the waters whereof no sooner gushed forth than the stream was swallowed up in a small opening of the same ground which gave it birth. There were besides in the mountain, which was full of cavities, many habitable places, in which were seen, now rough with rust, anvils and hammers for stamping money. The place, Egyptian writers relate, was a secret mint at the time of Antony's union with Cleopatra.

6. Accordingly, regarding his abode as a gift from God, he fell in love with it, and there in prayer and solitude spent all the rest of his life. The palm afforded him food and clothing. And, that no one may deem this impossible, I call to witness Jesus and His holy angels that I have seen and still see in that part of the desert which lies between Syria

and the Saracens' country, monks of whom one was shut up for thirty years and lived on barley bread and muddy water, while another in an old cistern (called in the country dialect of Syria Gubba) kept himself alive on five dried figs a day. What I relate then is so strange that it will appear incredible to those who do not believe the words that "all things are possible to him that believes."

7. But to return to the point at which I digressed. The blessed Paul had already lived on earth the life of heaven for a hundred and thirteen years, and Antony at the age of ninety was dwelling in another place of solitude (as he himself was wont to declare), when the thought occurred to the latter, that no monk more perfect than himself had settled in the desert. However, in the stillness of the night it was revealed to him that there was farther in the desert a much better man than he, and that he ought to go and visit him. So then at break of day the venerable old man, supporting and guiding his weak limbs with a staff, started to go: but what direction to choose he knew not. Scorching noontide came, with a broiling sun overhead, but still he did not suffer himself to be turned from the journey he had begun. Said he, "I

Three biographies - Saint Jerome

believe in my God: some time or other He will show me the fellow-servant whom He promised me." He said no more. All at once he beholds a creature of mingled shape, half horse half man, called by the poets Hippocentaur. At the sight of this he arms himself by making on his forehead the sign of salvation, and then exclaims, "Holloa! Where in these parts is a servant of God living?" The monster after gnashing out some kind of outlandish utterance, in words broken rather than spoken through his bristling lips, at length finds a friendly mode of communication, and extending his right hand points out the way desired. Then with swift flight he crosses the spreading plain and vanishes from the sight of his wondering companion. But whether the devil took this shape to terrify him, or whether it be that the desert which is known to abound in monstrous animals engenders that kind of creature also, we cannot decide.

8. Antony was amazed, and thinking over what he had seen went on his way. Before long in a small rocky valley shut in on all sides he sees a mannikin with hooked snout, horned forehead, and extremities like goats' feet. When he saw this, Antony like a good soldier seized the shield of

faith and the helmet of hope: the creature none the less began to offer to him the fruit of the palm-trees to support him on his journey and as it were pledges of peace. Antony perceiving this stopped and asked who he was. The answer he received from him was this: "I am a mortal being and one of those inhabitants of the desert whom the Gentiles deluded by various forms of error worship under the names of Fauns, Satyrs, and Incubi. I am sent to represent my tribe. We pray you in our behalf to entreat the favour of your Lord and ours, who, we have learned, came once to save the world, and 'whose sound has gone forth into all the earth.'" As he uttered such words as these, the aged traveller's cheeks streamed with tears, the marks of his deep feeling, which he shed in the fulness of his joy. He rejoiced over the Glory of Christ and the destruction of Satan, and marvelling all the while that he could understand the Satyr's language, and striking the ground with his staff, he said, "Woe to you, Alexandria, who instead of God worshippest monsters! Woe to you, harlot city, into which have flowed together the demons of the whole world! What will you say now? Beasts speak of Christ, and you instead of God worship monsters." He had not finished speaking when, as if on wings, the wild creature fled away. Let no one scruple to believe this incident; its truth is supported by what took place when Constantine was on the throne, a matter of which the whole world was witness. For a man of that kind was brought alive to Alexandria and shown as a wonderful sight to the people. Afterwards his lifeless body, to prevent its decay through the summer heat, was preserved in salt and brought to Antioch that the Emperor might see it.

9. To pursue my proposed story. Antony traversed the region on which he had entered, seeing only the traces of wild beasts, and the wide waste of the desert. What to do, whither to wend his way, he knew not. Another day had now passed. One thing alone was left him, his confident belief that he could not be forsaken by Christ. The darkness of the second night he wore away in prayer. While it was still twilight, he saw not far away a she-wolf gasping with parching thirst and creeping to the foot of the mountain. He followed it with his eyes; and after the beast had disappeared in a cave he drew near and began to look within. His curiosity profited nothing: the darkness hindered vision. But, as the Scripture says, perfect love casts out fear. With halting step and bated breath he entered, carefully feeling his

way; he advanced little by little and repeatedly listened for the sound. At length through the fearful midnight darkness a light appeared in the distance. In his eager haste he struck his foot against a stone and roused the echoes; whereupon the blessed Paul closed the open door and made it fast with a bar. Then Antony sank to the ground at the entrance and until the sixth hour or later craved admission, saying, "Who I am, whence, and why I have come, you know. I know I am not worthy to look upon you: yet unless I see you I will not go away. You welcome beasts: why not a man? I asked and I have found: I knock that it may be opened to me. But if I do not succeed, I will die here on your threshold. You will surely bury me when I am dead."

Such was his constant cry: unmoved he stood. ? To whom the hero thus brief answer made

"Prayers like these do not mean threats; there is no trickery in tears. Are you surprised at my not welcoming you when you have come here to die?" Thus with smiles Paul gave him access, and, the door being opened, they threw themselves into each other's arms, greeted one another by name, and joined in thanksgiving to God.

Three biographies - Saint Jerome

10. After the sacred kiss Paul sat down and thus began to address Antony. "Behold the man whom you have sought with so much toil, his limbs decayed with age, his gray hairs unkempt. You see before you a man who ere long will be dust. But love endures all things. Tell me therefore, I pray you, how fares the human race? Are new homes springing up in the ancient cities? What government directs the world? Are there still some remaining for the demons to carry away by their delusions?" Thus conversing they noticed with wonder a raven which had settled on the bough of a tree, and was then flying gently down till it came and laid a whole loaf of bread before them. They were astonished, and when it had gone, "See," said Paul, "the Lord truly loving, truly merciful, has sent us a meal. For the last sixty years I have always received half a loaf: but at your coming Christ has doubled his soldier's rations."

11. Accordingly, having returned thanks to the Lord, they sat down together on the brink of the glassy spring. At this point a dispute arose as to who should break the bread, and nearly the whole day until eventide was spent in the discussion. Paul urged in support of his view the rites of

hospitality, Antony pleaded age. At length it was arranged that each should seize the loaf on the side nearest to himself, pull towards him, and keep for his own the part left in his hands. Then on hands and knees they drank a little water from the spring, and offering to God the sacrifice of praise passed the night in vigil. At the return of day the blessed Paul thus spoke to Antony: "I knew long since, brother, that you were dwelling in those parts: long ago God promised you to me for a fellow-servant; but the time of my falling asleep now draws nigh; I have always longed to be dissolved and to be with Christ; my course is finished, and there remains for me a crown of righteousness. Therefore you have been sent by the Lord to lay my poor body in the ground, yea to return earth to earth."

12. On hearing this Antony with tears and groans began to pray that he would not desert him, but would take him for a companion on that journey. His friend replied: "You ought not to seek your own, but another man's good. It is expedient for you to lay aside the burden of the flesh and to follow the Lamb; but it is expedient for the rest of the brethren to be trained by your example. Wherefore be so good as to go and fetch the

cloak Bishop Athanasius gave you, to wrap my poor body in." The blessed Paul asked this favour not because he cared much whether his corpse when it decayed were clothed or naked (why should he indeed, when he had so long worn a garment of palm-leaves stitched together?); but that he might soften his friend's regrets at his decease. Antony was astonished to find Paul had heard of Athanasius and his cloak; and, seeing as it were Christ Himself in him, he mentally worshipped God without venturing to add a single word; then silently weeping he once more kissed his eyes and hands, and set out on his return to the monastery which was afterwards seized by the Saracens. His steps lagged behind his will. Yet, exhausted as he was with fasting and broken by age, his courage proved victorious over his years.

13. At last wearied and panting for breath he completed his journey and reached his little dwelling. Here he was met by two disciples who had begun to wait upon him in his advanced age. Said they, "Where have you stayed so long, father?" He replied, "Woe to me a sinner! I do not deserve the name of monk. I have seen Elias, I have seen John in the desert, and I have really

seen Paul in Paradise." He then closed his lips, beat upon his breast, and brought out the cloak from his cell. When his disciples asked him to explain the matter somewhat more fully he said, "There is a time to keep silence, and a time to speak." (Ecclesiastes 3:7)

14. He then went out, and without taking so much as a morsel of food returned the same way he came, longing for him alone, thirsting to see him, having eyes and thought for none but him. For he was afraid, and the event proved his anticipations correct, that in his absence his friend might yield up his spirit to Christ. And now another day had dawned and a three hours' journey still remained, when he saw Paul in robes of snowy white ascending on high among the bands of angels, and the choirs of prophets and apostles. Immediately he fell on his face, and threw the coarse sand upon his head, weeping and wailing as he cried, "Why do you cast me from you, Paul? Why go without one farewell? Have you made yourself known so late only to depart so soon?"

15. The blessed Antony used afterwards to relate

that he traversed the rest of the distance at such speed that he flew along like a bird; and not without reason: for on entering the cave he saw the lifeless body in a kneeling attitude, with head erect and hands uplifted. The first thing he did, supposing him to be alive, was to pray by his side. But when he did not hear the sighs which usually come from one in prayer, he fell to kisses and tears, and he then understood that even the dead body of the saint with duteous gestures was praying to God unto whom all things live.

16. Then having wrapped up the body and carried it forth, all the while chanting hymns and psalms according to the Christian tradition, Antony began to lament that he had no implement for digging the ground. So in a surging sea of thought and pondering many plans he said: If I return to the monastery, there is a four days' journey: if I stay here I shall do no good. I will die then, as is fitting, beside Your warrior, O Christ, and will quickly breathe my last breath. While he turned these things over in his mind, behold, two lions from the recesses of the desert with manes flying on their necks came rushing along. At first he was horrified at the sight, but again turning his thoughts to God, he waited without alarm, as

though they were doves that he saw. They came straight to the corpse of the blessed old man and there stopped, fawned upon it and lay down at its feet, roaring aloud as if to make it known that they were mourning in the only way possible to them. Then they began to paw the ground close by, and vie with one another in excavating the sand, until they dug out a place just large enough to hold a man. And immediately, as if demanding a reward for their work, pricking up their ears while they lowered their heads, they came to Antony and began to lick his hands and feet. He perceived that they were begging a blessing from him, and at once with an outburst of praise to Christ that even dumb animals felt His divinity, he said, "Lord, without whose command not a leaf drops from the tree, not a sparrow falls to the ground, grant them what you know to be best." Then he waved his hand and bade them depart. When they were gone he bent his aged shoulders beneath the burden of the saint's body, laid it in the grave, covered it with the excavated soil, and raised over it the customary mound. Another day dawned, and then, that the affectionate heir might not be without something belonging to the intestate dead, he took for himself the tunic which after the manner of wicker-work the saint had woven out of palm-leaves. And so returning to the monastery he unfolded everything in order to his disciples, and on the feast-days of Easter and Pentecost he always wore Paul's tunic.

17. I may be permitted at the end of this little treatise to ask those who do not know the extent of their possessions, who adorn their homes with marble, who string house to house and field to field, what did this old man in his nakedness ever lack? Your drinking vessels are of precious stones; he satisfied his thirst with the hollow of his hand. Your tunics are of wrought gold; he had not the raiment of the meanest of your slaves. But on the other hand, poor though he was, Paradise is open to him; you with all your gold will be received into Gehenna. He though naked yet kept the robe of Christ; you, clad in your silks, have lost the vesture of Christ. Paul lies covered with worthless dust, but will rise again to glory; over you are raised costly tombs, but both you and your wealth are doomed to the burning. Have a care, I pray you, at least have a care for the riches you love. Why are even the grave-clothes of your dead made of gold? Why does not your vaunting cease even amid mourning and tears? Cannot the carcasses of rich men decay except in silk?

18. I beseech you, reader, whoever you may be, to remember Jerome the sinner. He, if God would give him his choice, would much sooner take Paul's tunic with his merits, than the purple of kings with their punishment.

Three biographies - Saint Jerome

Limovia.net - classics of Christianity

Look for other classics of Christianity on: *LIMOVIA.NET*

THANK YOU!

Printed in the USA
CPSIA information can be obtained
at www.ICGtesting.com
LVHW010938011023
759816LV00017B/1508